INTRODUCTION TO

Four Essential Elements
of
Christian Maturity

Andrew Wommack

Published in partnership between Andrew Wommack Ministries and Harrison House Publishers

Woodland Park, CO 80862 - Shippensburg, PA 17257

ISBN 13 TP: 978-1-6675-0241-0

ISBN 13 eBook: 978-1-6675-0242-7

For Worldwide Distribution, Printed in the USA

1 2 3 4 5 6 / 25 24 23 22

Contents

Introduction
5

Become a Living Sacrifice
7

Renew Your Mind
12

Receive the Holy Spirit's Power
20

Understand Your New Identity
37

Receive Jesus as Your Savior
48

Receive the Holy Spirit
50

Call for Prayer
52

About the Author
53

Introduction

Growing in the Lord is something most, if not every, Christian wants to do. I'm not aware of anyone who wants to stay a baby. But in talking with many, I can tell you they are not maturing.

What does it take to become a mature Christian? You might think it's some long, toilsome process and that you never really know when you get there. People would say, "You just can't know when you've matured. It's prideful to say you can know when you get there." Well, defining what it means to be mature could be subjective, but did you know that it's something God *wants* you to know? There are basic elements in the Word of God that guarantee you are maturing if you apply them to your life. And here's the good news: your growth will be automatic!

Before I get into sharing these elements, I want to encourage you with one more thing: as you're reading through this material, remember to be as smart as a cat! You know, if you rub it the wrong way, against the grain, all of its hair stands up. To solve the problem, you just turn the cat around and keep rubbing. So, as I'm dealing with helping you grow and mature, what I share may rub you the wrong way. If it does, just turn around—repent—and keep reading. It'll go to feeling good. These elements have changed my life, and I know they will do the same for you!

Become a
Living Sacrifice

Let's start in Romans 12:1 which says, *"I beseech you therefore, brethren, by the mercies of God, that ye present your bodies a living sacrifice, holy, acceptable unto God, which is your reasonable service."*

This isn't just for the super saint; this is for every born-again believer. God wants you to present your body as a living sacrifice. If you couple this verse with the next one, it says you will prove what is the *"good, and acceptable, and perfect, will of God"* (v. 2). That means that part of the process of proving His will is predicated upon you becoming a living sacrifice. In other words, you would have to backslide on God to keep from maturing. It would just be automatic, if you are totally surrendered to the Lord.

What does it mean to truly be a living sacrifice? Simply put, it means you have to die to yourself. That may sound like a cliché to you, but let me say it this way: to begin to mature in the Lord, you have to realize that self is your worst enemy. That might not make you feel good, but I am telling you the truth in love (Eph. 4:15). It's not really the devil or other people who are keeping you from maturity. It's you!

Look what Paul said:

> *But none of these things move me, neither count I*
> *my life dear unto myself, so that I might finish my*
> *course with joy, and the ministry, which I have*
> *received of the Lord Jesus, to testify the gospel of*
> *the grace of God.*

Acts 20:24

This is one of the secrets to Paul's life: He did not count his life dear unto himself! As a matter of fact, he went on to write, *"But God forbid that I should glory, save in the cross of our Lord Jesus Christ, by whom the world is crucified unto me, and I unto the world"* (Gal. 6:14). Paul was dead to the world. How do you insult or hurt a dead man? If he's truly dead, you can't do it.

Becoming a living sacrifice is part of what a mature Christian is. You have no chance of ever reaching maturity as long as you are sitting on the throne of your life. The way up in God's kingdom is down. If you want to advance, you have to humble yourself. James 4:6 says,

"God resisteth the proud, but giveth grace unto the humble."

Pride doesn't necessarily mean arrogant. In its simplest form, it's just self-centeredness. Self is one of the first hurdles you've got to cross to become a living sacrifice. But at the end of self is the beginning of God.

You have no
chance of ever
reaching maturity
as long as you are
sitting on the throne
of your life.

The problem with a living sacrifice is that it keeps wanting to crawl off the altar! It's going to take a conscious effort on your part to deny yourself as Jesus said (Matt. 16:24). That means it won't be a one-time decision. You'll have to decide every single day to run up the white flag and say, "God, it's all about You. I present myself as a living sacrifice on the altar, and I'm asking for Your fire to fall and consume me." It'll be worth it!

Self is one of the first hurdles you've got to cross to become a living sacrifice.

Renew Your Mind

The second element to maturity is right from the same passage where I shared the first element, in Romans 12. The second verse says,

"And be not conformed to this world: but be ye transformed by the renewing of your mind, that ye may prove what is that good, and acceptable, and perfect, will of God."

You've got to renew your mind to the Word of God, or it will be dangerous for you to only be a living sacrifice. Satan can come along and prey upon your willingness to do whatever you think is God's good, acceptable, and perfect will. Because it sounds or seems good, you'll do it, and it'll get you in a mess.

The word "conformed" in Romans 12:2 means "to fashion alike" (*Strong's Concordance*), which is to be poured into the mold of. In other words, don't let the world's thinking mold you. Don't be easy prey for the devil to come along and deceive you. You must know the truth of God's Word in order for His thinking to become your thinking.

The word "transformed" in this same verse is the Greek word *metamorphoo*. It's where we get the word "metamorphosis" from, which is the process of how a caterpillar spins a cocoon and comes out as a butterfly. This is saying

You must know the
truth of God's Word
in order for His
thinking to become
your thinking.

that if you want transformation like this, it comes through renewing your mind to the Word of God.

Look at this parable Jesus gave:

> *So is the kingdom of God, as if a man should cast seed into the ground; And should sleep, and rise night and day, and the seed should spring and grow up, he knoweth not how. For the earth bringeth forth fruit of herself; first the blade, then the ear, after that the full corn in the ear. But when the fruit is brought forth, immediately he putteth in the sickle, because the harvest is come.*

Mark 4:26–29

The seed is symbolic of the Word of God and the effect it has in your life. The ground is symbolic of your heart. The word for "herself" is from the Greek word *automatos*, and it's from where we get "automatic" and "automatically." The earth brings forth fruit automatically. I cannot overstate this. If you would simply plant God's Word in your heart and do this consistently over a period of time, it would change you automatically. There are no exceptions. It never fails.

The seed of God's Word is dependable (Ps. 119:89). It's incorruptible (1 Pet. 1:23). If you aren't seeing it produce in your life, it's not the seed that's the problem; it's the ground—your heart. You've either got a hardened heart, or

If you would simply
plant God's Word
in your heart…, it
would change you
automatically.

you're caught up in the cares of this life, or you're being moved by persecution. To cleanse your heart of these, you have to give yourself to the Word. You must meditate in it day and night, as it says in Joshua 1:8—

"This book of the law shall not depart out of thy mouth; but thou shalt meditate therein day and night, that thou mayest observe to do according to all that is written therein: for then thou shalt make thy way prosperous, and then thou shalt have good success."

It's a lack of meditating on the Word day and night that prevents you from prospering and having good success. It's an unrenewed mind that keeps you from proving the good, acceptable, and perfect will of God.

Now, some people hear what I'm saying and think, *This is awesome! I'm going to take God's Word and plant it today!* But if they don't see total transformation within two or three days, they say, "Well, it didn't work. I tried it." That's like a woman who has a physical relationship with a man and is disappointed when she doesn't deliver a baby in just a few days. That's not how it works. Most women don't even know they're pregnant until weeks after conception. In the same way, you've got to give the Word time to germinate in your heart before you know that it's working.

You can't wait until a crisis situation and then spend all night praying and fasting for something to happen quickly. I don't care how badly you want a child today; you aren't

You can't wait until a crisis situation and then spend all night praying and fasting for something to happen quickly.

going to have one if you haven't conceived months before. In the natural, people understand this principle, but in the spiritual, the vast majority of the body of Christ is violating it all of the time. They're praying for results, but they haven't planted the Word of God in their hearts. When things don't work out or they get worse, they wonder, *Why hasn't God done anything?* Not smart.

There are steps to renewing our minds that we can't skip, or things just won't work. It's *"first the blade, then the ear, after that the full corn in the ear"* (Mark 4:28), or it's the good, then the acceptable, and then the perfect will of God, as we read in Romans 12.

It takes a commitment to mix the Word of God with faith in order to see this process through (Heb. 4:2). But if you'll do this over a prolonged period of time, it'll produce *"some thirtyfold, some sixty, and some an hundred"* (Mark 4:20b). The only thing you need is a seed—a catalyst—to start this process. That's the Word of God. You take the Word, plant it, protect it in your heart by meditating in it, mix it with faith, and it'll absolutely transform you by the renewing of your mind. You will grow and mature.

If you're wondering what your next step should be, I want to encourage you to shut down anything you can to spend as much time as possible in the Word of God. Maybe you need to come to Charis Bible College to be in a concentrated environment where you can sit under the Word for two years. I guarantee, you'll come out of here stronger than horseradish! This is how simple it is. People make change a traumatic experience. They'll say things like, "Well, my situation is unique." It's not. The Scripture says,

> *There hath no temptation taken you but such as is common to man: but God is faithful, who will not suffer you to be tempted above that ye are able; but will with the temptation also make a way to escape, that ye may be able to bear it.*
>
> 1 Corinthians 10:13

Any time you get to thinking your situation's different and you need special consideration because the Word just won't work for you, you are in deception. Your devil isn't any worse than anybody else's devil. It's not true. You just take the Word of God and meditate in it day and night, and it'll transform you!

Receive the Holy Spirit's Power

You cannot mature on your own. Despite your best intentions, you'll only be attempting it out of the flesh. Look how Jesus responded to those who, by all appearances, seemed to be approaching things the right way.

> *Now when he was in Jerusalem at the Passover, in the feast day, many believed in his name, when they saw the miracles which he did. But Jesus did not commit himself unto them, because he knew all men, And needed not that any should testify of man: for he knew what was in man.*
>
> John 2:23–25

This is very revealing. These people had concluded that Jesus was the Messiah. They were ready to follow Him. But He didn't commit Himself to them, which is an Old English way of saying He did not want them to represent Him. Why not? Because He knew they would've been doing it out of their human ability and nature.

I tell you, Jesus' mindset was so contrary to how we see Him represented today. We use gimmicks, smoke and mirrors, tight jeans, and whatever else to attract people. We preach little sermonettes that make little Christianettes, which aren't making an impact on the world. We teach, "Well, people are basically good." But that's not the way Jesus thought. Man, left to himself, is not good.

Quoting from Psalms, Paul wrote,

> *There is none who does good, no, not one.*
>
> Romans 3:12b

Over in Jeremiah, it says,

> *O Lord, I know that the way of man is not in himself: it is not in man that walketh to direct his steps.*
>
> Jeremiah 10:23

> *The heart is deceitful above all things, and desperately wicked: who can know it?*
>
> Jeremiah 17:9

The truth is, Jesus did not want them representing Him because they needed the Holy Spirit, who hadn't come yet. You see, the Christian life is not just difficult to live; it's impossible to live without the power of the Holy Spirit.

Jesus said,

> *It is the spirit that quickeneth; the flesh profiteth nothing.*

> John 6:63a

The ministry of the Holy Spirit is specifically designed to take you beyond the limits of the flesh and help you grow and mature. The disciples understood this after Jesus had been resurrected. They had the greatest news the world had ever heard, and yet Jesus basically told them, "Don't go anywhere. Don't you tell anyone what you've seen until you receive the power of the Holy Spirit" (Luke 24:46–48 and Acts 1:4–8). That is nearly mind-boggling! But it should be Christ living through you by the power of the Holy Spirit.

To me, one of the most amazing passages of Scripture in the entire Bible is found in John 16:7, where Jesus said,

> *Nevertheless I tell you the truth; It is expedient for you that I go away: for if I go not away, the Comforter will not come unto you; but if I depart, I will send him unto you.*

> John 16:7

The word "expedient" means it is to our advantage. It is actually better for us that Jesus left and sent the Holy Spirit. What a statement! Most Christians would not agree with

The Christian
life is not just
difficult to live; it's
impossible to live
without the power of
the Holy Spirit.

that. They'd much rather have Jesus in His physical body right here today.

I've got a booklet titled *10 Reasons It's Better to Have the Holy Spirit*, and this is by no means a complete list. But I want to talk about five of them here.

Five Reasons It's Better to Have the Holy Spirit

1. The first thing is that Jesus can now live inside of us by the Holy Spirit. During His earthly ministry, Jesus was limited by His physical body and couldn't be in multiple places at once. If we wanted Him to minister to us, we had to find Him first. Then, once we got there, we would have to press through the crowd. If we were able to do all of that, He would minister to us, and it would be awesome. Then we'd go our separate ways. We might remember what He preached and we might not. If we wanted Him to minister to us again, we'd have to do the whole thing all over again. But now the Scripture says,

   Now if any man have not the Spirit of Christ, he is none of his.

   Romans 8:9b

It also says,

> *God hath sent forth the Spirit of his Son into your hearts, crying, Abba, Father.*

Galatians 4:6b

Jesus is inside of every born-again believer! He is always with us through the indwelling Holy Spirit (1 Cor. 12:3 and 1 John 4:2). This is one reason that having the Holy Spirit is better than having Jesus in His physical body.

When Satan killed Jesus, he thought he'd won. But then Jesus rose from the dead! On the day of Pentecost, 120 "little Jesuses" came out of the upper room, when the Holy Spirit came upon them (Acts 2:4). They started ministering and three thousand other people were born again (Acts 2:41). Then, a couple of weeks later, five thousand people were saved (Acts 4:4). The dumbest thing Satan ever did was kill Jesus. Only heaven will tell how many times Jesus has been multiplied in believers since the first century.

2. The second reason it's better to have the Holy Spirit is that when you receive Jesus as your Lord and are saved, you are born of the Spirit, of God. There are so many scriptures that talk about this. Here are a few:

Jesus answered and said unto him, Verily, verily, I say unto thee, Except a man be born again, he cannot see the kingdom of God.

John 3:3

That which is born of the flesh is flesh; and that which is born of the Spirit is spirit.

John 3:6

But as many as received him, to them gave he power to become the sons of God, even to them that believe on his name: Which were born, not of blood, nor of the will of the flesh, nor of the will of man, but of God.

John 1:12–13

Whosoever believeth that Jesus is the Christ is born of God.

1 John 5:1a

Before, you *"were by nature [a child] of wrath, even as others"* (Eph. 2:3b), but now that you are born again, you are by nature a child of God! Your old nature is gone! You have a born-again spirit and are totally revolutionized on the inside. A lot of Christians believe they have a sinful nature alongside their born-again nature, but that isn't true. You have only one nature:

> *Therefore if any man be in Christ, he is a new creature: old things are passed away; behold, all things are become new.*
>
> 2 Corinthians 5:17

Now, as I shared before, you just need to renew your mind to who you are in the spirit. I'll talk more on that later.

3. The third reason it's better with the Holy Spirit is that without Him, you just can't perceive spiritual things.

It says in 1 Corinthians 2:14,

> *But the natural man receiveth not the things of the Spirit of God: for they are foolishness unto him: neither can he know them, because they are spiritually discerned.*

The Word of God is spiritually discerned. It's written to your heart, not to your head. I'm not saying you should

You have a
born-again spirit
and are totally
revolutionized
on the inside.

turn your brain off when you're trying to renew your mind. But you can't perceive the Word with just human understanding; it has to be revealed unto you by the Holy Spirit.

Over in 1 Corinthians 2:9, it says,

Eye hath not seen, nor ear heard, neither have entered into the heart of man, the things which God hath prepared for them that love him.

This is a quotation from Isaiah 64:4. Most modern-day Christians will take this and say, "Well, you just can't understand the things of God. Further along, we'll know. Further along, we'll understand." But the next verse says,

But God hath revealed them unto us by his Spirit.

1 Corinthians 2:10a

There were two times that Jesus told His disciples that the Holy Spirit would reveal things to them:

But the Comforter, which is the Holy Ghost, whom the Father will send in my name, he shall teach you all things, and bring all things to your remembrance, whatsoever I have said unto you.

John 14:26

Howbeit when he, the Spirit of truth, is come, he will guide you into all truth: for he shall not

You can't perceive the Word with just human understanding; it has to be revealed unto you by the Holy Spirit.

speak of himself; but whatsoever he shall hear, that shall he speak: and he will shew you things to come.

John 16:13

The Holy Spirit will literally make the Bible come alive on the inside of you. I tell you, any good thing that's ever happened in my life is because of that! If you do not understand what I'm talking about, the Word hasn't become alive to you. You've got to desire it. You've got to open your heart and ask, "Holy Spirit, reveal the Word of God to me."

4. The fourth reason it's better to have the Holy Spirit is that when He comes upon you, you receive miracle-working power. This is the baptism of the Holy Spirit, which is mentioned throughout the New Testament. As I mentioned, Jesus told His disciples not to do anything until they had received power:

Behold, I send the promise of my Father upon you: but tarry ye in the city of Jerusalem, until ye be endued with power from on high.

Luke 24:49

But ye shall receive power, after that the Holy Ghost is come upon you: and ye shall be witnesses unto me both in Jerusalem, and in all Judaea, and in Samaria, and unto the uttermost part of the earth.

Acts 1:8

If you want to see the miraculous power of God in your life, you need the baptism of the Holy Spirit. There's not a single person who saw miracles happen in their ministry who did not teach this. Yet there are a lot of people today preaching against the Holy Spirit, saying, "That all passed away." That's wrong.

Mark 16:20 says,

> *And they went forth, and preached every where, the Lord working with them, and confirming the word with signs following.*

God confirmed the preaching of His Word with miracles, and He's still doing that today. He hasn't changed (Mal. 3:6). That's what the baptism of the Holy Spirit produces.

If you want to see what your spirit is like, you have to look into the Word of God.

5. Now, the fifth reason it's better to have the Holy Spirit goes along with the fourth one. When you receive the baptism of the Holy Spirit, it includes speaking in tongues!

> *And they were all filled with the Holy Ghost, and began to speak with other tongues, as the Spirit gave them utterance.*

> Acts 2:4

This is the most common gift you will see accompanying the infilling of the Holy Spirit in the book of Acts. It's a gift God wants you to have, and I want to briefly share with you why.

It says in 1 Corinthians 14:14,

> *For if I pray in an unknown tongue, my spirit prayeth, but my understanding is unfruitful.*

Your spirit is the part of you that was born again, that was completely changed. It has the mind of Christ (1 Cor. 2:16). It knows all things (1 John 2:20). But how do you access this knowledge? It's not meant to remain in your spirit. The Bible says that when you pray in tongues, your spirit is speaking the hidden wisdom of God (1 Cor. 2:7). Therefore, when you speak in tongues, you are drawing out this wisdom and knowledge.

Now, as it says, your understanding will be unfruitful when you pray in tongues, which means that you won't understand what you're saying. That's why it says "*pray that [you] may interpret*" (1 Cor. 14:13). In other words, just ask God to reveal what you're saying. The rest of the Christian life is learning how to renew your mind and draw out what's in your spirit. Speaking in tongues and interpreting it is an essential part of that. It's one of the most important things you can ever do.

I'm telling you, there's so much more to the Christian life when you have the Holy Spirit. Most people just don't fully appreciate what God has given them. But you cannot fully mature without the baptism of the Holy Spirit and utilizing what He makes available to you. You are missing out on one of the greatest things that God has given you to promote spiritual growth. You've got to have it, and you've got to be speaking in tongues on a regular basis. That's quite a claim. But that's my testimony, and I'm sticking with it.

There's so much more to the Christian life when you have the Holy Spirit.

Understand Your New Identity

The thing that really changed my life was 2 Corinthians 5:17, where it says, *"Therefore if any man be in Christ, he is a new creature: old things are passed away; behold, all things are become new."*

When I first came across this verse, I prayed, "God, I know I am in Christ. I know my life has been changed. I have a relationship with You. I know I'm saved, but my life hasn't changed. There are still all kinds of problems. This verse doesn't match what I see in the natural, so how can this be?" Then the Lord led me to 1 Thessalonians 5:23—

> *And the very God of peace sanctify you wholly; and I pray God your whole spirit and soul and body be preserved blameless unto the coming of our Lord Jesus Christ.*

When I read that, the Holy Spirit revealed to me that I had a spirit, soul, and body. Up until that time, I'd only had a concept of the body and soul. It was obvious what the body is. It's the part that interacts with the physical world. It's constantly updating me about how it's doing. Through my five senses, it's giving me information about the world around me. That was easy to understand.

I also understood that there's an inner part that can't physically interact with the world. For instance, if someone was to say something that touched my feelings, that would be my soul, my mental-emotional part. It would take place in the soulish realm.

However, I didn't know what the spirit was, this third part Scripture was talking about. If it's distinct from what I can see and feel, how can I know what's true about it? What is the spirit? Most people would totally draw a blank at these questions. It's one of the reasons they haven't grown or matured.

Jesus answered it this way,

> *It is the spirit that quickeneth; the flesh profiteth nothing: the words that I speak unto you, they are spirit, and they are life.*

John 6:63

God's Word is spirit! If you want to see what your spirit is like, you have to look into the Word of God. James 1:23–25 says,

> *For if any be a hearer of the word, and not a doer, he is like unto a man beholding his natural face in a glass: For he beholdeth himself, and goeth his*

way, and straightway forgetteth what manner of
man he was. But whoso looketh into the perfect
law of liberty, and continueth therein, he being
not a forgetful hearer, but a doer of the work, this
man shall be blessed in his deed.

The Word of God is a spiritual mirror. It perfectly reflects who you are in the spirit. It's the only way you can tell who you are in the spirit. The Bible says your spirit has love, joy, peace, longsuffering, gentleness, goodness, faith, meekness, and temperance (Gal. 5:22–23). Somebody will say, "Well, I don't believe that because I don't feel it." See, they're trying to discern who they are in the spirit through their soul, by their emotions. Your emotions won't tell you what's true in the spirit. The only way to access the spirit is through the Word of God. This is what changed my life!

If you think what the Word says, you will always have love, joy, and peace coming out of your spirit. Anytime you're discouraged, anytime you're fearful, it's because somehow or another, you're letting thoughts other than the Word dominate you. As you think in your heart, that's the way you're going to be (Prov. 23:7).

Imagine that your mind is like a valve with a pipe between your spirit and your body. The only thing stopping what God has put in your spirit from coming into the physical realm is your mind. It's the control. So, in order to

If you want to see
what your spirit is
like, you have to
look into the
Word of God.

turn on the valve and get things flowing, you have to renew your mind to what the Word says.

It would be impossible to be depressed if you think what the Word says about you. The Word says your spirit only produces love, joy, and peace. There's nothing wrong with your emotions. There's <u>something</u> wrong with your <u>focus</u>. Whatever you focus on is going to dominate you. And if you are depressed, it's because you've been thinking on depressing things.

I learned that the key to the Christian life is to quit going by what I feel and what things look like. I just hold up the spiritual mirror of God's Word to see how I am. Ephesians 1:3 says,

> *Blessed be the God and Father of our Lord Jesus Christ, who hath blessed us with all spiritual blessings in heavenly places in Christ.*

If you ask me how I'm doing, I'll say, "I'm blessed." As I conform my thinking to what the Word says, I begin to experience all of this blessedness.

Here is another example: The Bible says that you are the righteousness of God in Christ Jesus (2 Cor. 5:21). Ephesians 4:24 says,

> *And that ye put on the new man, which after God is created in righteousness and true holiness.*

Notice, this is not saying that you are becoming righteous. No, you were *created* that way! You are as righteous—in right standing with God—as you will ever be. Your spirit is perfect. It's identical to Jesus. The Bible says that *"as he is, so are we in this world"* (1 John 4:17b). But if you think, *I'm not like Jesus. I'm just an old sinner saved by grace*, then that's the way you're going to feel and act. It becomes a self-fulfilling prophecy. All the while, this righteousness will stay trapped in your spirit. But when you realize that you *were* an old sinner but now are saved by grace, then the righteousness of God will come out of your spirit into your body and your soul.

When I started living out of the spirit and finding out who I was in Christ, it radically changed my life.

Some people say, "Well, I can accept that I was that way when I got born again, but I've messed up things since then." Ephesians 1:13 says that *"after that ye believed, ye were sealed with that holy Spirit of promise."* The way the word "sealed" is used here means your spirit is vacuum packed. You have a seal around it that keeps it from impurities. If you sin as a Christian, it will never contaminate your spirit.

"What happens when I sin, then?" someone will ask. Most Christians, when they sin, get right into telling God what a failure they are. But that's not worshiping Him in spirit and in truth (John 4:24); it's worshiping Him in the flesh. And the Bible says that those who are in the flesh cannot please God (Rom. 8:8). You don't turn to the flesh

The key to the Christian life is to quit going by what I feel and what things look like.

after you've sinned; you turn your attention back to what the Word says, to what's true in your born-again spirit! What I'm saying is not just a better way. It's the only way. You can't approach God in your own self.

Now, when you sin, it gives Satan an inroad into your life. You're yielding yourself to him. And John 10:10 says that *"the thief cometh not, but for to steal, and to kill, and to destroy."* Satan is out to destroy you. He's out to make you sick. He's out to make you poor. He's out to make you depressed and fearful. If you go live in sin, Satan will eat your lunch and pop the bag. But in your spirit, you have been perfected forever (Heb. 10:14). When I saw that, it set me free *from* sin, not *to* sin. It set me free from the guilt and the condemnation associated with sin.

You've got the same power on the inside of you that raised Jesus Christ from the dead. Look at this passage:

> *The eyes of your understanding being enlightened; that ye may know what is the hope of his calling, and what the riches of the glory of his inheritance in the saints, And what is the exceeding greatness of his power to us-ward who believe, according to the working of his mighty power, Which he wrought in Christ, when he raised him from the dead, and set him at his own right hand in the heavenly places, Far above all principality, and power, and might, and dominion, and every*

name that is named, not only in this world, but
also in that which is to come.

Ephesians 1:18–21

What you have in the spirit is infinitely greater than whatever problem you've got in the natural. In the spirit, you are one awesome person. You can choose to go by the spirit or by what you can see, taste, hear, smell, and feel. The apostle Paul wrote,

> *While we look not at the things which are seen,*
> *but at the things which are not seen: for the things*
> *which are seen are temporal; but the things which*
> *are not seen are eternal.*

2 Corinthians 4:18

Choose to look at the eternal. Choose to go by who you are in the spirit. Walk by faith and not by sight (2 Cor. 5:7). When I went by what God's Word says about me, I started doing things that I could never have done. I was an introvert. I couldn't look at a person in the face. But when I saw that I was exactly like Jesus in my spirit, I understood that the works that He did, I can do also (John 14:12). I started talking like it. I started acting like it. I didn't see anything, and I didn't feel anything, but I believed it. Now I talk to millions of people every day. I've seen blind eyes open, deaf ears open, and people raised from the dead. Awesome things happened when I found out who I am.

If you go live in sin,
Satan will eat your
lunch and pop
the bag.

It's encouraging, once you understand this, because even when you blow it, you can just retreat into who you are in Christ. <u>You won't lose any momentum</u>!

The elements I've shared in this book are how I went from being a babe in Christ to maturity. If you'll do the things I've explained, they will help you grow too!

Let me pray for you:

> Father, I'm releasing my faith and believing that the Holy Spirit reveals the elements I've shared in this book so that the person reading this book might grow and mature. Help them to be humble and recognize the importance of becoming a living sacrifice, renewing their mind, receiving the baptism of the Holy Spirit, and knowing who they are in Christ. May they get hold of these truths and meditate on them until they explode on the inside of them. Thank You, Jesus!

Receive Jesus as Your Savior

Choosing to receive Jesus Christ as your Lord and Savior is the most important decision you'll ever make!

God's Word promises, *"That if thou shalt confess with thy mouth the Lord Jesus, and shalt believe in thine heart that God hath raised him from the dead, thou shalt be saved. For with the heart man believeth unto righteousness; and with the mouth confession is made unto salvation"* (Rom. 10:9–10). *"For whosoever shall call upon the name of the Lord shall be saved"* (Rom. 10:13). By His grace, God has already done everything to provide salvation. Your part is simply to believe and receive.

Pray out loud: "Jesus, I confess that You are my Lord and Savior. I believe in my heart that God raised You from the dead. By faith in Your Word, I receive salvation now. Thank You for saving me."

The very moment you commit your life to Jesus Christ, the truth of His Word instantly comes to pass in your spirit. Now that you're born again, there's a brand-new you!

Please contact us and let us know that you've prayed to receive Jesus as your Savior and to receive some free materials to help you on your new journey. Call our Help-line: **719-635-1111** (available 24 hours a day, seven days a week) to speak to a staff member who is here to help you understand and grow in your new relationship with the Lord.

Welcome to your new life!

Receive the Holy Spirit

As His child, your loving heavenly Father wants to give you the supernatural power you need to live a new life. *"For every one that asketh receiveth; and he that seeketh findeth; and to him that knocketh it shall be opened…how much more shall your heavenly Father give the Holy Spirit to them that ask him?"* (Luke 11:10–13).

All you have to do is ask, believe, and receive!

Pray this: "Father, I recognize my need for Your power to live a new life. Please fill me with Your Holy Spirit. By faith, I receive it right now. Thank You for baptizing me. Holy Spirit, You are welcome in my life."

Congratulations! Now you're filled with God's supernatural power.

Some syllables from a language you don't recognize will rise up from your heart to your mouth (1 Cor. 14:14). As you speak them out loud by faith, you're releasing God's power from within and building yourself up in the spirit (1 Cor. 14:4). You can do this whenever and wherever you like.

It doesn't really matter whether you felt anything or not when you prayed to receive the Lord and His Spirit. If you believed in your heart that you received, then God's Word promises you did. *"Therefore I say unto you, What things soever ye desire, when ye pray, believe that ye receive them, and ye shall have them"* (Mark 11:24). God always honors His Word—believe it!

Please let us know that you've prayed to be filled with the Holy Spirit and to receive some free materials we have for you. We would like to rejoice with you and help you understand more fully what has taken place in your life. Call our Helpline: **719-635-1111** (available 24 hours a day, seven days a week).

Call for Prayer

If you need prayer for any reason, you can call our Prayer Line 24 hours a day, seven days a week at 719-635-1111. A trained prayer minister will answer your call and pray with you. Every day, we receive testimonies of healings and other miracles from our Prayer Line, and we are ministering God's nearly-too-good-to-be-true message of the Gospel to more people than ever. So I encourage you to call today!

About the Author

ANDREW WOMMACK'S life was forever changed the moment he encountered the supernatural love of God on March 23, 1968. As a renowned Bible teacher and author, Andrew has made it his mission to change the way the world sees God.

Andrew's vision is to go as far and deep with the Gospel as possible. His message goes far through the *Gospel Truth* television program, which is available to nearly half the world's population. The message goes deep through discipleship at Charis Bible College, headquartered in Woodland Park, Colorado. Founded in 1994, Charis has campuses across the United States and around the globe.

Andrew also has an extensive library of teaching materials in print, audio, and video—most of which can be accessed for free from his website: awmi.net.

CONTACT INFORMATION

Andrew Wommack Ministries Inc.

PO Box 3333

Colorado Springs, CO 80934-3333

Email: info@awmi.net

Helpline: 719-635-1111

Helpline available 24/7

Website: www.awmi.net

Andrew's LIVING COMMENTARY BIBLE SOFTWARE

Andrew Wommack's *Living Commentary* Bible study software is a user-friendly, downloadable program. It's like reading the Bible with Andrew at your side, sharing his revelation with you verse by verse.

Main features:
- Access to Windows, Mac, and web versions
- Andrew Wommack's notes on over 25,000 Scriptures and counting
- 11 Bible versions, 5 commentaries, 3 concordances, and 2 dictionaries
- Maps and charts
- User notes
- Enhanced text selection and copying
- Commentaries and charts
- Scripture-reveal and note-reveal functionalities
- "Living" (i.e., constantly updated)
- Quick navigation
- Robust search capabilities
- Automatic software updates
- Mobile phone and tablet support for web version
- Screen reader support for visually impaired users (Windows version)
- Bonus material

Whether you're new to studying the Bible or a seasoned Bible scholar, you'll gain a deeper revelation of the Word from a grace-and-faith perspective.

Purchase Andrew's *Living Commentary* today at **awmi.net/living**, and grow in the Word with Andrew.

Item code: 8350

ANDREW WOMMACK MINISTRIES

Box-set curriculum!

CHARIS
HEALING
UNIVERSITY

The *Charis Healing University* box-set curriculum is made up of extensive teaching and guided application from trusted Bible teachers Andrew Wommack, Barry Bennett, Carlie Terradez, Carrie Pickett, Daniel Amstutz, Duane Sheriff, and Greg Mohr.

Charis Healing University contains over 60 hours of teaching spread across **forty-eight online video lessons**, six Q&A panel discussions, and several study resources that have been organized into three different sections:

- *Expect* will build your faith to believe for healing.
- *Experience* will help you know success and receive your healing.
- *Empower* will equip you to minister healing to others with confidence.

The *Charis Healing University* box-set curriculum includes **workbooks** for each section, a **USB** containing audio lessons, and access to our **online course**. The online course gives you access to video lessons and printable PDFs for group study.

Go to **awmi.net/HealingU** or call **719-635-1111**.

Item Code: 6012-U

Your peace doesn't have to ebb and flow with the tides of circumstance. Build your life on the solid foundation of the Word.

Visit our website for teachings, videos, testimonies, and other resources that will encourage you with truth for any situation and help you learn God's plan for relationships, finances, faith, and more.

"I was lost deep in the world. . . . I started seeking the truth, and through AWM's resources, I have been set free . . . including receiving miracles of finances when everything seemed impossible. I am at peace with myself. I thank AWM for sharing the truth, which has freed me to understand God."

— David M.

Be empowered to live the victorious life God intended for you! Visit **awmi.net** to access our library of free resources.

Teaching God's unconditional love and grace.

CHARIS
BIBLE COLLEGE

God has **more** for you.

Are you longing to find your God-given purpose? At Charis Bible College you will establish a firm foundation in the Word of God and receive hands-on ministry experience to **find, follow,** and **fulfill** your purpose.

Scan the QR code for a free Charis teaching!

CharisBibleCollege.org
Admissions@awmcharis.com
(844) 360-9577

Change your life. **Change the *world.***

A single drop
of water seem[...]
insignificant...u[...]
it joins with ma[...]
others to crea[...]
a river, ocean[...]
or flood. Our
partners are lik[...]
those many dro[...]
of water, joinin[...]
together to floo[...]
the earth with t[...]
living water of t[...]
Gospel.

Without *you*, there is no *us*.

Because of our partners, we are able to:

➤ Teach God's Word through TV, live streams, and conferences broadcast worldwide

➤ Train and equip Charis students around the world to pastor, teach, and disciple

➤ And so much more!

When you partner with Andrew Wommack Ministries, you are reaching lives far beyond your personal sphere. Join us in sharing the Gospel as far and as deep as possible.

Visit **awmi.net/grace** or call **719-635-1111** to become a Grace Partner today!

ANDREW WOMMACK MINISTRIES

Don't miss
The Gospel Truth
with Andrew Wommack!

Discover God's unconditional love and grace
and see God in a whole new way!

▶ Hear the Word of God taught
with simplicity and clarity.

▶ Understand the true Gospel
message and be set free
from all kinds of bondages.

▶ Learn how to receive
your breakthrough.

Go to **awmi.net/video** for local
broadcast times or to watch online.

AWM Offices

We'd love to hear from you!
Reach out to us at any of our offices near you.

Andrew Wommack Ministries USA
Headquarters—Woodland Park, CO
Website: awmi.net
Email: info@awmi.net

Andrew Wommack Ministries Australia
Website: awmaust.net.au
Email: info@awmaust.net.au

Andrew Wommack Ministries Canada
Website: awmc.ca
Email: info@awmc.ca

Andrew Wommack Ministries France
Website: awmi.fr
Email: info@awmi.fr

Andrew Wommack Ministries Germany
Website: andrewwommack.de
Email: info@andrewwommack.de

Andrew Wommack Ministries Hong Kong
Website: awmi.hk
Email: info@awmi.hk

Andrew Wommack Ministries Hungary
Website: awme.hu
Email: hungary@awme.net

Andrew Wommack Ministries Indonesia
Website: awmindonesia.net
Email: awmindonesia@gmail.com

Andrew Wommack Ministries India
Website: awmindia.net
Email: info@awmindia.net

Andrew Wommack Ministries Italy
Website: awme.it
Email: info@awme.it

Andrew Wommack Ministries Lithuania
Website: awmi.lt
Email: charis@charis.lt

Andrew Wommack Ministries Netherlands
Website: andrewwommack.nl
Email: info.nl@awmcharis.com

Andrew Wommack Ministries Poland
Website: awmpolska.com
Email: awmpolska@zyciesozo.com

Andrew Wommack Ministries Russia
Website: cbtcrussia.ru
Email: info@cbtcrussia.ru

Andrew Wommack Ministries South Africa
Website: awmsa.net
Email: enquiries@awmsa.net

Andrew Wommack Ministries Uganda
Website: awmuganda.net
Email: awm.uga@awmcharis.com

Andrew Wommack Ministries United Kingdom
Website: awme.net
Email: enquiries@awme.net

Andrew Wommack Ministries Zimbabwe
Website: awmzim.net
Email: enquiries@awmzim.net

For a more comprehensive list of all of
our offices, visit **awmi.net/contact-us**.

Connect with us on social media.